Dr. Seuss Workbook
CURSIVE

There are few things as fun as the fabulous thrill of learning and using a brand-new skill!

Welcome to Dr. Seuss Workbooks, where kids learn and practice important skills they'll use in the classroom and beyond! Grab a pen or pencil and get ready to explore cursive writing.

Learners will practice all the lowercase letters first, but not in alphabetical order. Instead, letters are grouped by the lines and curves that form them.

Most activities focus on one letter at a time, providing practice writing letters by themselves and then as parts of words and sentences. When cursive letters are written together to form a word, the lines forming them are connected.

Start by reviewing the correct way to hold a pen or pencil.

left-handed   right-handed

Help your child become familiar with our "dot and arrow" steps to write letters and numbers.

Each black dot (•) indicates the beginning of a new line, where the pen should leave the page to make a separate stroke. The arrows (➡) show the direction of pen movement. Strokes without dots indicate a continuation and change of direction.

Come trace, draw, and learn cursive writing with us.

–Your friends at Dr. Seuss

Get ready to write cursive letters by tracing these lines.
Start at each dot and follow the arrows without lifting your hand.

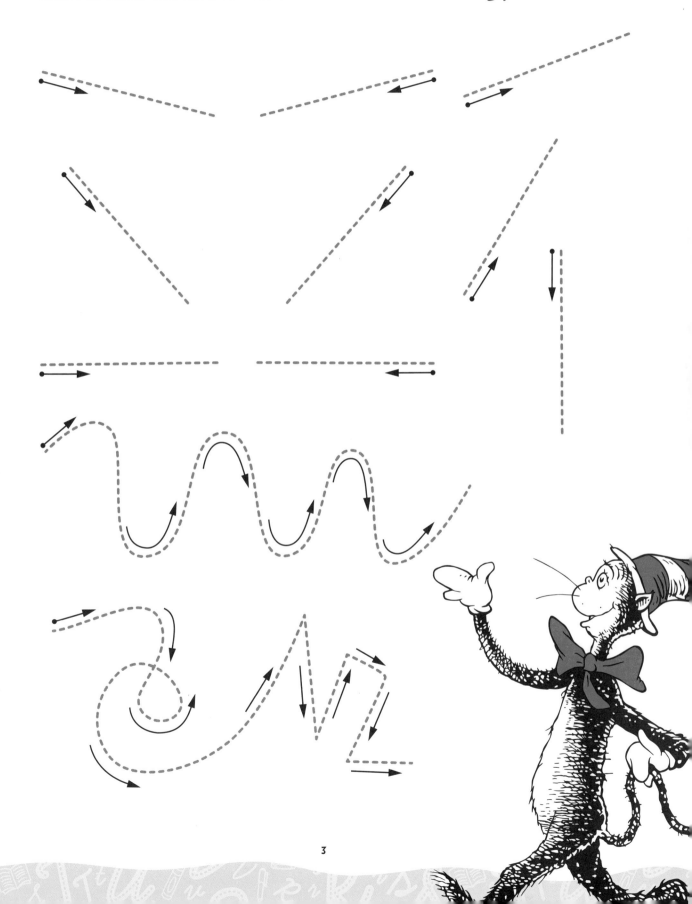

Loops and Lines!

Trace each curve. Then draw it again by yourself.

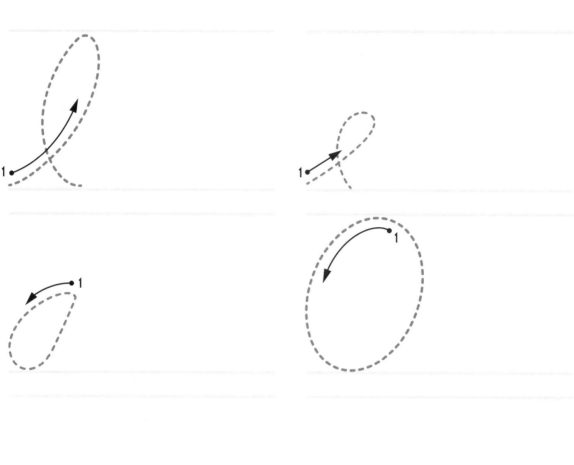

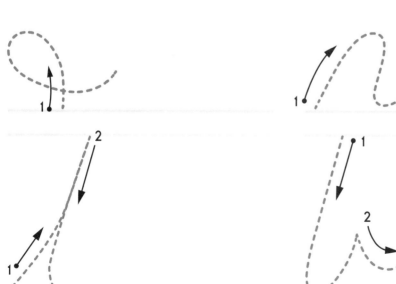

Trace this big looping path from **START** to **END**. But wait!
Say the alphabet aloud as you pass each letter.

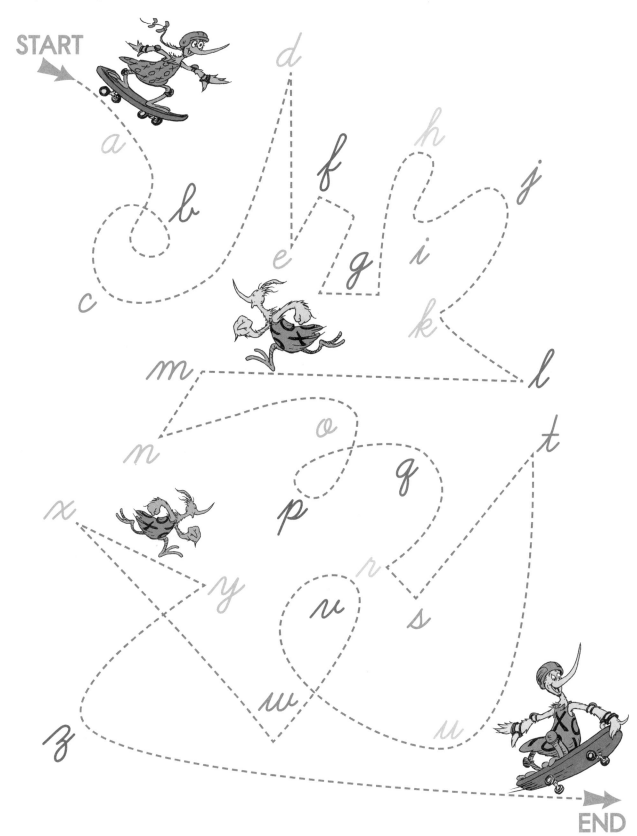

START

END

Show What You Know

Trace each group of uppercase and lowercase letters.
Then say the letter aloud as you look at the cursive form.

Mm *Mm* Nn *Nn*

Oo *Oo* Pp *Pp*

Qq *Qq* Rr *Rr*

Ss *Ss* Tt *Tt*

Uu *Uu* Vv *Vv*

Ww *Ww* Xx *Xx*

Yy *Yy* Zz *Zz*

Lowercase c and a

Trace, then write

c   c   c

Trace, then write each word.

cat

cactus

circus

Trace this phrase. Then write it.

cook a carrot cake

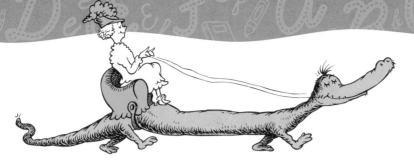

Trace, then write *a*.

a a

Trace, then write each word.

alligator

artwork

airplane

Trace this phrase. Then write it.

an actor ate apples

Lowercase d and g

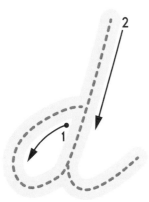

Trace, then write *d*.

d d

Trace, then write each word.

drip

drum

diamond

Trace this phrase. Then write it.

do a dragon dance

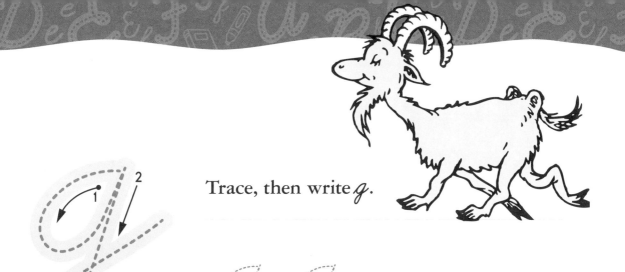

Trace, then write *g*.

g g

Trace, then write each word.

gate

garage

goat

Trace this phrase. Then write it.

go get a giant gerbil

Let's Review

Trace, then write each word.

cage

giraffe

iguana

angry

Trace and write this word.
Then write a new word using
these letters in reverse order.
Draw a picture of your new
word in the box on the right.

gab

Trace every letter. Then look for the names of six animals hidden in this word search. Write them at the bottom of the page.

e	d	g	c	a	t
a	d	o	g	a	c
g	t	i	g	e	n
l	b	a	m	e	l
e	n	a	t	a	g
c	g	g	b	a	t

Lowercase i and t

3

2

1

Trace, then write *i*.

i i

Trace, then write each word.

ice

iguana

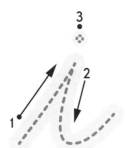

ink

Trace this phrase. Then write it.

it is incredibly itchy

Trace, then write *t*.

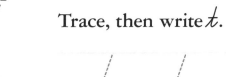

Trace, then write each word.

tennis

track

table

Trace this phrase. Then write it.

Lowercase p and u

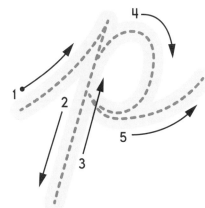

Trace, then write *p*.

p p

Trace, then write each word.

potato

pig

puppy

Trace this phrase. Then write it.

please pass the pie

Trace, then write *u*.

Trace, then write each word.

umbrella

urchin

upset

Trace this phrase. Then write it.

use ugly underwear

Lowercase q and j

Trace, then write *q*.

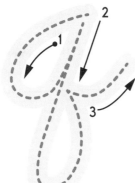

q q

Trace, then write each word.

quiet

quarter

quack

Trace this phrase. Then write it.

the quilt queen quit

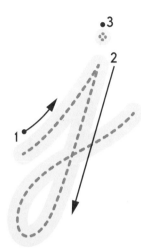

Trace, then write *j*.

j j

Trace, then write each word.

juice

jellyfish

jump

Trace this phrase. Then write it.

jiggle a jar of jam

You Can Write, All Right!

Trace all the words. Then draw lines between the ones that match.

soup   pizza

taco   pasta

pizza   soup

pasta   taco

t p g
i u
y m i
l h
f a e
o c
b r
n s
j k
d

Unscramble the crossed-out letters to spell a secret message.

___ ___ ___ ___   ___ ___

___ ___ ___ ___

Follow this trail. Then read the letters
you crossed and write the words they
make in the space below.

START

END

Lowercase e and l

Trace, then write *e*.

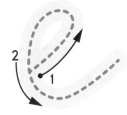

Trace, then write each word.

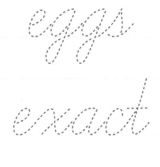

eggs

exact

edge

Trace this phrase. Then write it.

every emu escaped

Trace, then write *l*.

Trace, then write each word.

loud

liquid

leaves

Trace this phrase. Then write it.

little lions like limes

Lowercase f and h

Trace, then write *f*.

f f

Trace, then write each word.

feet

fix

fish

Trace this phrase. Then write it.

five fans feel funny

Trace, then write *h*.

𝒽 *h h*

Trace, then write each word.

huge

hungry

hurry

Trace this phrase. Then write it.

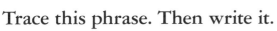

his hive had honey

A Secret Message!

Trace each word. Then cross out every one that has a match. Write the leftover words in the space at the bottom to reveal a message.

we

crab

shark

wave

shovel

decided

go

fish

not

sand

clam

to

shovel

fish

swim	clam
crab	sun
in	ship
wave	go
shark	the
ship	sand
lake	sun

Lowercase k and r

Trace, then write *k*.

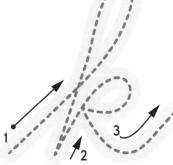

k k

Trace, then write each word.

kettle

kite

kind

Trace this phrase. Then write it.

kittens kept kidding

Trace, then write *n*.

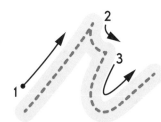

Trace, then write each word.

rabbit

rake

rumble

Trace this phrase. Then write it.

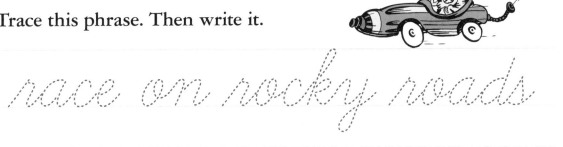

race on rocky roads

Lowercase s and b

Trace, then write s.

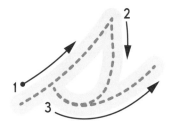

s s

Trace, then write each word.

scuba

skip

safe

Trace this phrase. Then write it.

she saw a shark

Trace, then write *b*.

bb

Trace, then write each word.

banana

brown

baby

Trace this phrase. Then write it.

a big balloon burst

Lowercase o and v

Trace, then write *o*.

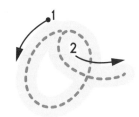

o o

Trace, then write each word.

ornament

orange

organize

Trace this phrase. Then write it.

old owls ordered oats

Trace, then write *u*.

Trace, then write each word.

violin

voice

nest

Trace this phrase. Then write it.

vans visited villages

What Do You A, B, C?

Write in cursive four things that you see in this scene.

Lowercase n and m

Trace, then write *n*.

Trace, then write each word.

mail

name

nickel

Trace this phrase. Then write it.

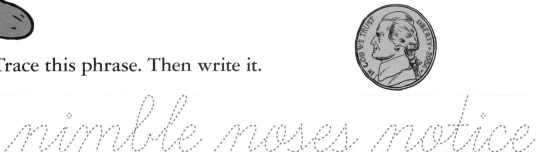

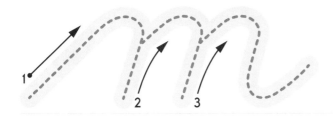

Trace, then write *m*.

m m m

Trace, then write each word.

money

monkey

mail

Trace this phrase. Then write it.

many maids march

Lowercase y and x

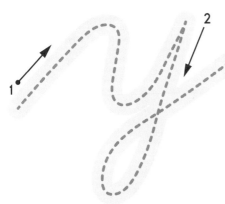

Trace, then write *y*.

Trace, then write each word.

yes

yawn

yam

Trace this phrase. Then write it.

your yam is yucky

Trace, then write *x*.

Trace, then write each word.

axe

oxen

mix

Trace this phrase. Then write it.

six foxes relax

Lowercase z and w

Trace, then write *z*.

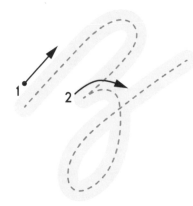

Trace, then write each word.

zipper

pizza

sizzle

Trace this phrase. Then write it.

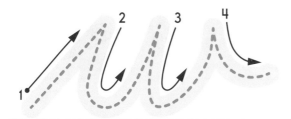

Trace, then write *w*.

w w w

Trace, then write each word.

walrus

wagon

whisk

Trace this phrase. Then write it.

wolves walked west

Let's Go Letters!

Trace, then write each word.

hungry

yummy

delicious

salty

Trace and write this word.
Then write a new word using
these letters in reverse order.
Draw a picture of your new
word in the box on the right.

stop

Trace every letter. Then look for the names of six foods hidden in this word search. Write them at the bottom of the page.

m	o	o	d	l	e
p	d	o	m	u	t
i	m	a	c	o	p
z	s	o	u	p	i
z	p	e	a	n	e
a	c	a	m	o	y

Wonderful Words

Trace all the words. Then draw lines between the ones that match.

moon   f   p   *yaun*

r   t   h

i   i

stars   g   n   i   *stars*

z   y

g   o   l

k   o   e

yaun   a   j   *sleep*

v   d

u   t

sleep   c   *moon*

Unscramble the crossed-out
letters to spell a secret message.

___ ___ ___ ___ ___ ___   ___ ___ ___ ___ ___ ___ ___ ___

Follow this trail. Then read the letters you crossed and write the words they make in the space below.

START

END

The Connection Challenge

Trace the word *start*. Then write a word in the next space that begins with the last letter of the word you just wrote. (We did the first few to show you how.) Now keep going until all the spaces are filled. Here's the catch: you can't repeat any words.

start

trap

pepper

Super Looper

Trace all these tricky lines without lifting your pencil.

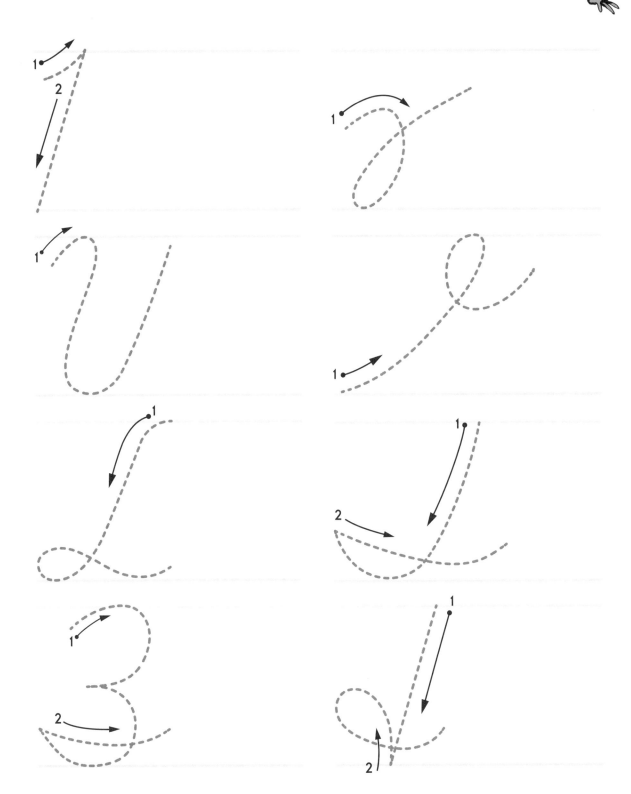

Trace the path from **START** to **END**. Say the letters aloud as you pass them.

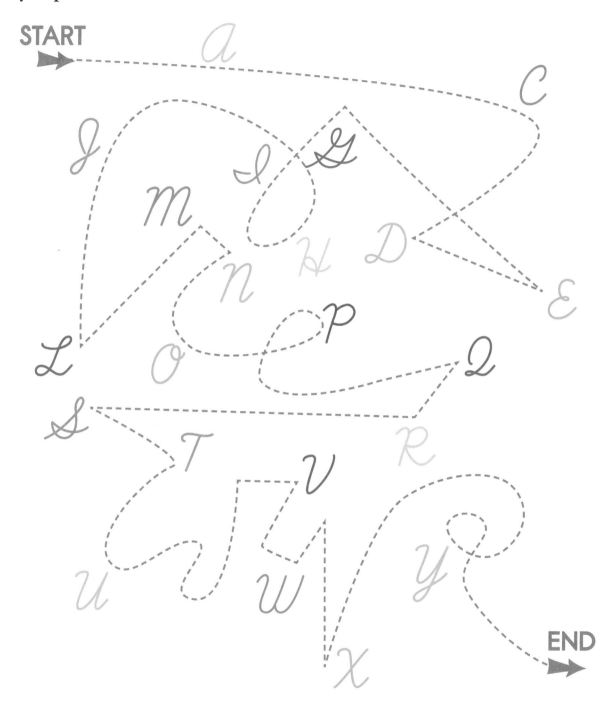

Wait! Which four letters are missing from the alphabet?

_____   _____   _____   _____

Uppercase A and C

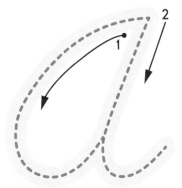 Trace, then write a.

Trace, then write each word.

Ape

Arrow

Anchor

Trace this phrase. Then write it.

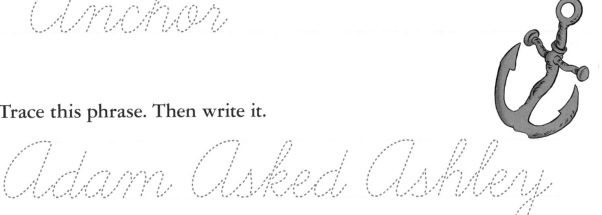

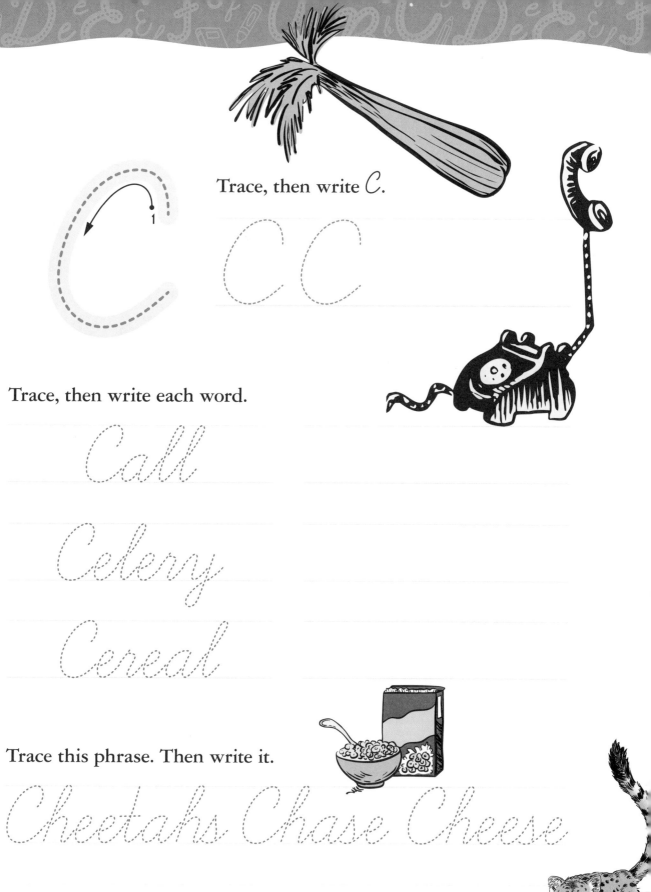

Trace, then write *C*.

Trace, then write each word.

Call

Celery

Cereal

Trace this phrase. Then write it.

Cheetahs Chase Cheese

Uppercase O and U

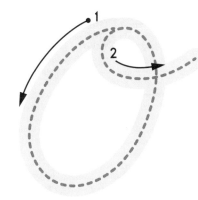

Trace, then write $\mathcal{O}$.

Trace, then write each word.

Over

Orbit

Oink

Trace this phrase. Then write it.

Trace, then write $\mathcal{U}$.

Trace, then write each word.

Useful

Untie

Upper

Trace this phrase. Then write it.

Use Uncle's Ukulele

Uppercase V and W

Trace, then write $\mathcal{V}$.

Trace, then write each word.

Vote

Voice

Velvet

Trace this phrase. Then write it.

View Violet Violins

Trace, then write $\mathcal{W}$.

Trace, then write each word.

Water

Western

Witch

Trace this phrase. Then write it.

Uppercase X and Y

1 → 2 → Trace, then write $\mathcal{X}$.

$\mathcal{X} \quad \mathcal{X} \mathcal{X}$

Trace, then write each word.

Xavier

Xmas

X-ray

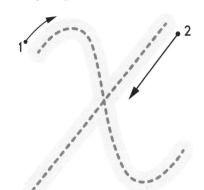

Trace this phrase. Then write it.

X-ray the Xylophone

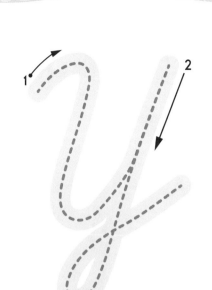

Trace, then write *Y*.

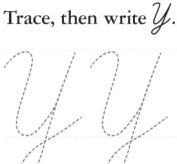

Y Y

Trace, then write each word.

Yertle

Yesterday

Young

Trace this phrase. Then write it.

Yellow Yaks Yawn

Practice with Punctuation

Trace, then write each punctuation mark three times.

.   ?

.   !

Use your new cursive skills to trace each word. Then create your own sentence.

Yesterday,

Did   ?

Look   !

Trace the words. Then add punctuation marks to make them complete sentences.

It was cold__

I went to the beach__

How many are there__

Are you afraid__

Oh__ Look at that__

What time is it__

Hey__ Where are you__

Hello__ Alice__

Uppercase P and Z

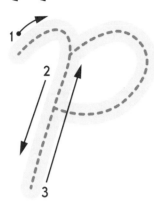

Trace, then write P.

Trace, then write each word.

Peter

Pants

Pauline

Trace this phrase. Then write it.

Peggy Picked Peppers

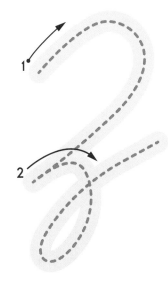

Trace, then write 𝓩.

𝓩 𝓩

Trace, then write each word.

𝓩ucchini

𝓩ip

𝓩inc

Trace this phrase. Then write it.

𝓩esty 𝓩ebras 𝓩oomed

Uppercase R and B

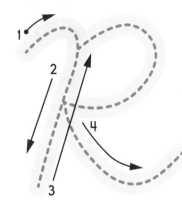

Trace, then write R.

Trace, then write each word.

Ring

Ranch

Rattle

Trace this phrase. Then write it.

Robert Roasted Roses

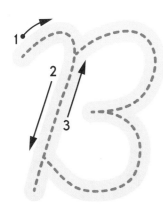

Trace, then write $\mathcal{B}$.

$\mathcal{B}\mathcal{B}$

Trace, then write each word.

$\mathcal{B}ush$

$\mathcal{B}ank$

$\mathcal{B}aby$

Trace this phrase. Then write it.

$\mathcal{B}illy~\mathcal{B}aked~\mathcal{B}read$

Uppercase H and K

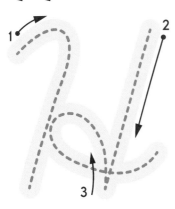

1 → 2
3 ↑

Trace, then write *H*.

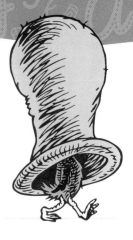

Trace, then write each word.

Hungry

House

Houston

Trace this phrase. Then write it.

Hang a Hat on Hal

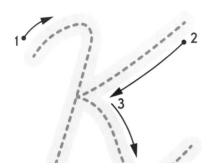 Trace, then write $\mathcal{K}$.

$\mathcal{K}$ $\mathcal{K}$ $\mathcal{K}$

Trace, then write each word.

Keep

Kitchen

Knife

Trace this phrase. Then write it.

Kelly Kissed a Knight

You Don't Say

Trace each word. Then cross out every one that has a match. Write the leftover words in the space at the bottom to reveal a message.

Car

Building

Sidewalk

Welcome

Bicycle

Bicycle

To

People

People

Road

Crowd

Car

Building

Busy

66

Crowd   Walk

Road   Store

Market   City

Sidewalk   Lights

Noise   Noise

Market   Store

Walk   Lights

Uppercase N and M

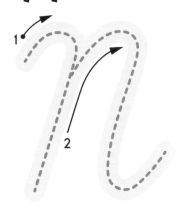

Trace, then write n.

Trace, then write each word.

Name

Never

November

Trace this phrase. Then write it.

Nine Newts Nibbled

Trace, then write *m*.

Trace, then write each word.

Michael

Machine

Middle

Trace this phrase. Then write it.

Make Many Mirrors

Uppercase F and J

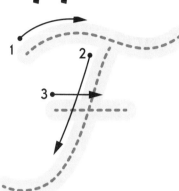

Trace, then write $\mathcal{F}$.

Trace, then write each word.

February

Frame

Fork

Trace this phrase. Then write it.

Frank Forgot Friday

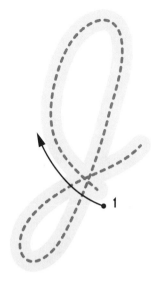

Trace, then write $\mathcal{J}$.

$\mathcal{J}$ $\mathcal{J}$

Trace, then write each word.

Jumble

Joy

Jamboree

Trace this phrase. Then write it.

Joey Just Jumped

71

Uppercase T and I

1• 2•

Trace, then write $\mathcal{T}$.

$\mathcal{T}$ $\mathcal{T}$ $\mathcal{T}$

Trace, then write each word.

Triangle

Termite

Thumb

Trace this phrase. Then write it.

Tim Trapped Ten Tigers

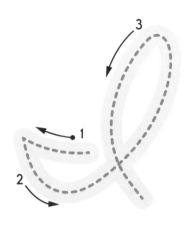

Trace, then write $\mathcal{I}$.

Trace, then write each word.

Imitate

Iron

Icing

Trace this phrase. Then write it.

Isabel Inspired Ideas

What's Happening?

Write in cursive four things you see in this scene.

Uppercase D and L

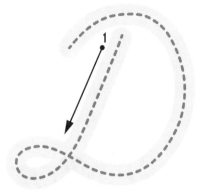

Trace, then write $\mathcal{D}$.

Trace, then write each word.

Dice

Dare

Declare

Trace this phrase. Then write it.

Danny Didn't Dance

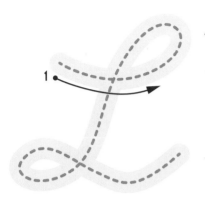

Trace, then write $\mathcal{L}$.

$\mathcal{L}$ $\mathcal{L}$ $\mathcal{L}$

Trace, then write each word.

Loop

Lost

Lullaby

Trace this phrase. Then write it.

Laughing Larry Left

Uppercase G and S

Trace, then write *G*.

Trace, then write each word.

Gate

Garlic

Grand

Trace this phrase. Then write it.

Gus Grows Grapes

Trace, then write $\mathcal{S}$.

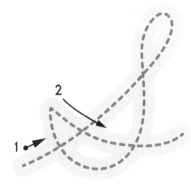

Trace, then write each word.

Soft

Salt

Sally

Trace this phrase. Then write it.

Sal Stole Sam's Socks

Uppercase E and Q

Trace, then write $\mathcal{E}$.

Trace, then write each word.

Ending

Earth

Easel

Trace this phrase. Then write it.

Eliza Elbowed Ellie

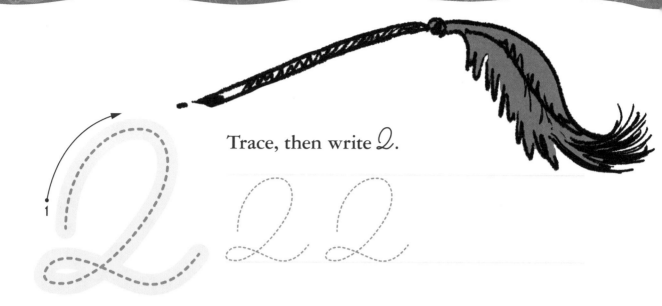

Trace, then write 𝒬.

𝒬 𝒬 𝒬

Trace, then write each word.

Quickly

Quality

Quill

Trace this phrase. Then write it.

Quentin Questioned

Moving Up to the Big Stuff

Trace, then write each word.

Decide

Laugh

Guess

Quiet

Trace and write this word.
Then write a new word using
these letters in reverse order.
Draw a picture of your new
word in the box on the right.

Part

Trace every letter. Then look for the names of six relatives hidden in this word search. Write them at the bottom of the page.

F	a	t	h	e	r
M	o	t	h	e	r
C	o	u	s	i	n
N	U	n	c	l	e
S	i	s	t	e	r
B	A	u	n	t	G

My Funny Friends

Pretend these are all people you know. Give each person a name and write it in the spaces below them. Make sure each name starts with a different letter of the alphabet. The first one has been done to show you how.

Annabel

Silly Story Starters

First, trace all the words you see.

Then, add words everywhere there is a blank space. There are hints above each space to help you out.

Once you're done, read your story to a friend.

noun

One day, a _____

verb

tried to _____

adjective

We were _____

verb

because it _____

verb

and _____ *, but*

verb

could not _____

Never give a

to a . If it

one of them,

it will never stop

. Also,

watch out for their

. They are

very .

What's in the Words?

Trace and write each of these words.

Street

Squirrel

Penny

Tree

Clouds

Surprise

Shout

Give

Now write in cursive four sentences that each contain at least one of those words.

Draw a picture about your story.

The Happy Hat Hut

Write in cursive four things you see in this scene.

Make Somebody Smile

Use your new cursive skills to create cards for your friends.
Write and trace them, color them, cut them out…and share!

Dear *Mikaela*,
I wish you were here!

Dear ———————————,
I wish you were here!

Best *friends*

Have a
Great
Day

You *Are*
Invited
to a
Party!

Words in the Wild

Draw a creature in each box. Then make up names for them.

ANSWERS

Pages 12–13

Pages 20–21

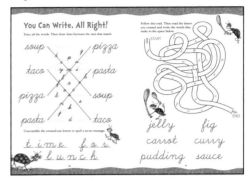

Pages 26–27

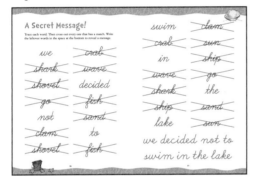

Pages 42–43

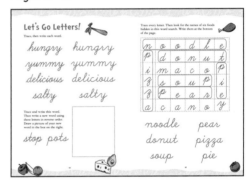

Pages 44–45

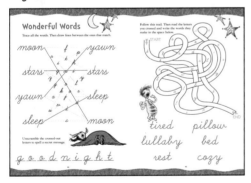

Page 49

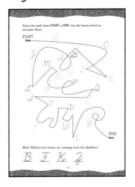

Page 59

Pages 66–67

Pages 82–83

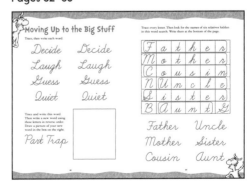

HOORAY FOR YOU

You learned something new.
With this brand-new skill,
there's so much you can do!

Show off your new skill by writing your name!

_____
NAME

is a

Cursive Champ!

CERTIFICATE OF ACHIEVEMENT